A Taste of Kentucky

A Taste of Kentucky

JANET ALM ANDERSON

THE UNIVERSITY PRESS OF KENTUCKY

Frontispiece: Fruits, vegetables, and meats in the
storage house of Mr. and Mrs. William S. Allen, near Barbourville,
November 1940. Photo by Marion Post Wolcott, Farm
Security Administration, Library of Congress.

Editorial and Sales Offices: Lexington, Kentucky 40506-0024

Library of Congress Cataloging-in-Publication Data

Anderson, Janet Alm, 1952-
   A Taste of Kentucky

   Bibliography: p.
   Includes index.
   1. Cookery, American—Southern style. 2. Food
habits—Kentucky. 3. Kentucky—Social life and
customs. I. Title.
TX715.A566416 1986   641.5   86-9197
ISBN 0-8131-1580-9

To my favorite
ethnogastronomist

JAY

With love

CONTENTS

ACKNOWLEDGMENTS

Thanks to Bob Turek, my first guide to archives and the planter of the seed which grew into this book.

Thanks to the many students, teachers, fieldworkers, and informants whose work has built the Western Kentucky University Folklife Archives into an invaluable regional folklife resource.

Thanks to the student and professional staff members whose labors have developed the Western Kentucky University Folklife Archives into a usable, working, and very accessible repository of cultural data. Among the student staff members, special thanks to Michele Kemp, Cliff Robinson, and Debbie Bays who assisted with this project.

Thanks to Beverly Brannan and Jerry Kearns of the Library of Congress Prints and Photographs Division for personal assistance beyond the call of duty.

Thanks to Connie Mills and Nancy Baird of the Kentucky Library for their help with photographs.

And thanks to Betty Elder for her continuing interest and advice.

A NOTE TO THE READER

The recipes, anecdotes, and sayings in this book all come from Kentucky. They are drawn from the collections of the Western Kentucky University Folklife Archives.

This outstanding regional folklife resource had its beginnings in the early 1950s, when faculty and students in folklore classes began to collect the folksongs, beliefs, and traditions of the counties surrounding Bowling Green and Western Kentucky University. In 1971 these individual collections of folklore materials were pooled to form an archive in support of the new graduate program in folk studies. Professional staff in Helm-Cravens Library developed the collection into an unusually accessible resource.

Today the Folklife Archives are housed in the Kentucky Building on the Western Kentucky University campus, and holdings include a wide range of materials: ethnographies, folksongs, epitaphs, beliefs, architectural documentation, political folklore, tape recorded music and interviews, and more. Over 2,000 fieldwork studies and more than 3,500 sound recordings form the basis of the archives' holdings.

Some of the material in this book is drawn from the Gordon Wilson Collection, the Wilgus Collection, and the Montell Belief Collection within the Folklife Archives. These collections were originally compiled by faculty members Gordon Wilson, D.K. Wilgus, and Lynwood Montell, each of whom is a nationally recognized folklorist and fieldworker. But most of the materials in these bodies of folklore data were collected by their students; indeed, all the collections in the Folklife Archives have been built on student work and continue to grow with the research and fieldwork of successive classes of graduate and undergraduate folklore students.

The Key to Sources on page 87 identifies the student collectors and their informants, whose work has formed the basis for this book.

All of the photographs in *A Taste of Kentucky* are believed to have been taken in Kentucky, although some locations and dates are unknown. Many pictures are from the collections of the Kentucky Library at Western Kentucky University. Some are from the Library of Congress and were taken in 1940 by Marion Post

Wolcott, a professional photographer working in Kentucky for the Farm Security Administration. Others are from the manuscript collections of the Western Kentucky University Folklife Archives; one is from Hutchins Library, Berea College; and a few were taken recently by me. The source of each is listed on page 94.

The recipes and recollections included here represent the food memories of many people, and were written down by field-workers over a span of nearly thirty years.

If you prepare any of these dishes, remember that because they were recorded in the field and frequently given from memory, the recipes are not necessarily accurate or complete. This book is not meant to be a comprehensive survey of Kentucky's characteristic or original dishes. The recipes, ancedotes, sayings, and photographs here are included because they are individually interesting; the assortment is offered as a sampling, a taste of Kentucky.

Today almost any family in Kentucky has easy access to supermarkets stocked with the products of thousands of farmers, scores of states, a variety of regions, and dozens of foreign countries. The shelves of grocery stores across the state hold fresh pineapples, frozen crab legs, pickled herring, artichokes, cashew nuts, dates, and fresh ginger root just waiting for the consumer with cash to spend. Spice counters display cinnamon, nutmeg, pepper, allspice, cloves, and even costly saffron. Cooks across the state plan and prepare dishes with ingredients purchased fresh, frozen, condensed, refrigerated, freeze-dried, dehydrated, reconstituted, evaporated, pickled, pressed, canned, bottled, and "vacuum-packed for sealed-in goodness." Through the advances of modern transportation and labor specialization, the cooks of Kentucky have the bounty of the world at their consumer fingertips.

The bread-winning role of the modern Kentuckian has shifted from grower, preserver, and preparer of foods to wage-earner in any of thousands of jobs and professions. Modern technology— mechanization, transportation, communication—has changed our lifestyle from that of subsistence farmers to specialist members of a cash economy. The traditional arts of gardening and food preservation have become nostalgic sidelines to modern life for many. A jar of home-canned tomatoes, a hickory-smoked ham, or a dish of watermelon pickles is no more a necessity of life for most Kentuckians than a mess of greens is necessary to stave off scurvy.

For Kentucky's earliest settlers, pouring through the Cumberland Gap and flat-boating down the Ohio River in the late 1700s, food was the focus of existence; the responsibility for meal-to-meal survival rested squarely on the shoulders of every settler. Subsistence was the occupation of the day, and menus were dictated strictly by availability of foodstuffs.

Kentucky's moderate temperatures, ample rainfall, and fertile soils welcomed the first settlers and provided a boon to their farming efforts. Crops take time, however, and while farms were begun, the region's abundant wild foods—deer, turkey, squirrel, greens, black walnuts, wild cherries, and more—provided the dishes on which settlers survived.

Kentucky's native people already supplemented a diet of wild offerings with cultivated pumpkins, corn, beans, and squash. The Scots and English, first European settlers to trek into the region, followed the Indians' lead with wild foods and soon planted their own pumpkins, beans, corn, turnips, potatoes, cucumbers, peas, and lettuce. These were combined with hogs for meat and cattle for beef and dairy products. Chickens provided both meat and eggs. Horseradish, sage, thyme, and mustard were soon planted, and fruit trees including apple, peach, pear, cherry, and plum were set out with hopes of rapid maturation.

Over 100,000 people crossed the Alleghenies through Cumberland Gap from 1775 to 1795 alone. As the natural offerings of the land diminished and cultivated crops increased, the settlers' dependence on wild food sources lessened. The transition from hunters and gatherers to farmers was in progress, and the limited diet of the earliest years was expanding.

Preservation of food, however, would continue to be a major concern and a critical enterprise for years to come. Even Kentucky's moderate climate dealt out a winter scarcity—no wild greens or berries, dormant gardens and fields, and less available game. The summer and fall bounty was carefully dried, pickled, smoked, and stored for the lean months of winter and early spring. Staples of the winter diet were the plentiful and easily dried corn and beans, while a well-stocked smokehouse provided country ham, jowl meat, pork shoulders, and bacon.

Pork, eaten fresh or preserved, was the favorite meat throughout the Kentucky region. Hog-butchering time arrived in the cold late fall weather, and people labored carefully through the processes of butchering, salting, drying, and smoking which would provide a favored foodstuff during the coming months.

By contrast, beef was preferred fresh and was butchered as the need arose. Cows also provided the prized dairy products—milk, buttermilk, cream, butter, and cheese. An excess of milk could even be converted to butter and sold for cash or traded.

With resources of both wild game and domesticated meats, Kentuckians never lacked for protein sources. The abundance of meat as well as dairy products gave the Kentucky pioneer a luxury of diet unavailable to the nearly vegetarian farmers of crowded and soil-poor Europe of the same period.

Another diet staple throughout Kentucky's early days was corn. This crop, which took well to Kentucky soil, was edible at almost any stage of its growth and provided an impressive array of dishes. Corn could be milled for flour, roasted, boiled, or baked. It could be served as hominy, grits, or mush, or it could be dried, parched, or pickled for winter use. Corn formed the basis of breads, porridges, cakes, a variety of vegetable dishes like corn pudding, ham—as feed for fattening hogs—and even the famous Kentucky corn whiskey.

Wheat does not grow well in newly cultivated soils, and for years wheat flour was expensive when it was available. Even after 1800 when wheat was in common production, the crop was valuable enough that it was often sold rather than consumed. Corn breads of many descriptions, from hoe cake to spoon bread, were the commonplace three-meals-a-day bread of life for Kentuckians.

A surplus of corn, too much to eat and too costly to transport, was converted into a major "cash crop," Kentucky corn whiskey. Aged in charred oak barrels, Kentucky's specialty known as bourbon was shortly an international success.

By the early 1800s Kentucky was no longer a frontier but a crossroads of an expanding nation. Luxury items including spices, linens, china, chocolate, coffee, and tea were becoming available through traders and merchants. Between 1800 and 1810 stagecoach travel became possible throughout the state, and 1811 marked the arrival of the first steamboat—soon to become a luxury mode of passenger transport. As transportation boomed, the possibilities for trade as well as for cash sales and purchases grew.

For farmers, transportation increased the opportunities for selling surplus goods, but farm families remained self-sufficient for years to come. Pickling, drying, and smoking were still critical to the feeding of a family. Commercial canning began in the early 1800s, and home canning in the recently patented glass jars spread rapidly after the turn of the twentieth century. Home canning methods progressed from open-kettle processing to waterbath canning and then pressure canning, each step increasing the safety and desirability of the product. The glass jars' visible contents stimulated an aesthetic interest in the art of food preservation and heightened the competition in county fairs and agricultural shows. In spite of improvements and advances, home food preservation was still a necessity in most families. It was not until well into the twentieth century that the availability of electricity lightened the farm wife's burden, allowing the cooling of the springhouse, icehouse, and root cellar to give way to the electric refrigerator and even the "deep freeze."

In the early 1920s, tractors began to replace horses and mules for farm work. Gradually mechanization spread through the farming scene as corn-pickers, pickup balers, hay crushers, potato combines, and cotton harvesters became the workhorses of the new century. In the days of a one-row, one-horse planter, a farmer could plant seven acres in a single day. Today's multi-row planters and speedy tractors can cover eighty to a hundred acres in the same time. Electrification brought improvements not only in food preservation and the domestic scene, but in agricultural technology as well. Innovations based on electricity brought electric water pumps, crop driers, automatic feeders, electric milking machines, greenhouse controls, and the warmth to hatch chicks. Production steadily rose, and the farmer's surplus cash from surplus sales rose with

it. The availability of transportation for crops also contributed to the transformation of the self-sufficient farmer into a cash consumer.

Today the majority of Kentuckians are employed in occupations which have no direct connection to the food production industry. Women, too, often work outside the home and contribute neither gardening skills nor food preservation knowledge to the feeding of the family. Instead, food-procurement skills are practiced in the marketplace. Food is produced elsewhere and transported directly into individual neighborhoods. In minutes, most Kentuckians can be dining "fast food" style on tacos, eggrolls, pepperoni pizza, or Whoppers.

Still—there's a lingering mystique about the melting taste of a fine country ham. There's something special about a mouthful of mutton barbeque, a vat of bubbling burgoo, or the minty whiff of a cool mint julep. There are hoe cakes, shucky beans, sassafras tea, apple stack cake, sorghum pie, and smooth Kentucky bourbon. And there's something—some pride or memory or self-knowledge—that will not let these Kentucky treasures fade.

A Taste of Kentucky

Smokehouse

Busy as a blind dog in a smokehouse.

Salt-Cured Ham

This is one recipe for the delicacy known as country ham. A salty-tasting final result is achieved through salting, smoking, and aging. No refrigeration is used in this process.

We salt our meat with just regular meat salt, and then it lays five weeks in that salt. Then we take it up and wash it with warm water and take borax and wash that salt and all off and it's pretty and white. Then I take a sprinkler with borax in it and sprinkle it all over that flesh side of that meat. And then we hang it up and let it dry and I smoke it with hickory bark. And it's got a hickory taste to it. And so it hangs up there till it dries. And while it's drying, I smoke it. Then I make sacks out of feed sacks. And I put them sacks over that bacon and tie it at the top with a string, you know. I tie it hard and tight, and by doing that you never have what I call a

Facing page: Kentucky gentlemen anticipate a savory end to their barbequing labors.

skipper bug. It's some kind of little black bug that lays eggs, and they hatch this little thing that looks like a worm. And if you've got them fixed that way, they'll never have none in it. While it's drying, it's smoking too, and then that keeps them off of it, you know. Well, when you put your meat bags on there and tie them up hard and tight, they can't get in there. And so I've not had a skipper on our bacon since we've been living up here, and we've been living here since 1937.

☐ Hettie Groce

Ham

This slow-cooker is a forerunner of today's crock pots.

Take cured ham. Boil in lard can two minutes for each pound of meat. Remove from heat. Place lard can in tub and place lid on can. Surround with old quilts and newspapers or anything to retain heat and leave until cool. Remove ham and serve.

☐ Rev. Wallace Morris

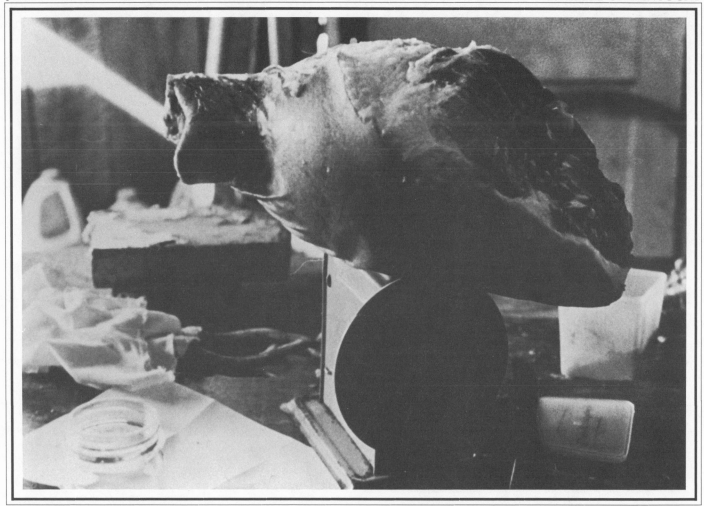

Country Ham and Red-Eye Gravy

A traditional accompaniment to country ham is red-eye gravy made of just two ingredients: ham drippings and coffee. If you look straight down into a round dish of gravy, you may see the red eye looking back at you.

1 large slice country ham
Cold water
Hot lard
1 tablespoon of flour
½ cup of strong coffee

In a pot, combine ham, water, and cover. Then soak it for about 3 hours and drain it and dry it. On a frying pan, combine hot lard and ham. Cook it slowly and keep turning it for about 15 minutes. Stir in the drippings and the coffee until it's thick. Then pour it on the ham.

□ Mrs. Pat Farra

Facing page: A twenty-pound piece of meat begins the curing process which will turn it into the prized Kentucky country ham. LaRue County, 1974.

Raising Meat to Eat

The first year me and Cord was married we had to buy everything we lived on. We bought meat that year, and that fall I bought sausage to cook of a morning. And then since then we have had our bacon both meat and lard. We've got meat now to last us to New Year's, lard too. We sold hams. Sold five, and them five hams brought a hundred and seventy-eight or nine dollars. We could have sold every bit of the meat we had this summer. You know, there ain't nobody on this road except maybe Aunt Mag who's got a hog to kill! Why, you know anybody could raise one hog and make their own bacon and their lard. Why I'd heap rather do that than go and buy this old chunk stuff, hadn't you?

□ Hettie Groce

Toothpick

If you pick your teeth with a splinter, you won't have a toothache.

The hog-butchering process begins in Metcalfe County.

Honesty

He's as honest as the cat when the meat is out of reach

Suckling Pig

The best pig to eat weighs about thirty-five pounds. Cut in half, hang him on a limb of a tree and build a fire under it. All the grease falls on the ground. That's the best.

□ Marshall Chatelain

Souse Meat

One way of reconstituting scraps into "meat" is to create this loaf of pickled souse or headcheese.

Boil head and feet of pig until tender. Pick meat off. Then boil meat in a mixture of vinegar, pepper, sage, and salt. To this add an amount of lard that equals one-fourth the weight of meat. Pour into a bowl and place a plate upside down on it with a flat iron on the plate. This keeps the fat from rising to the top and presses the meat and fat together. When the meat has become firm, it is ready to slice. Eat it on crackers with pepper.

□ Carl White

Pickled Pig's Feet

They'd usually kill about seven hogs each year. And of course we used to preserve the head and feet. Usually we'd make souse out of the head, but then we would pickle the pig's feet. You'd have to put them in salt, you know, just like—you'd have to salt them down, and I—Let's see, just how did we pickle the feet? I believe you'd have to put vinegar on them.

□ Alma Hughes

Fatback

Fatback is nothing but fat from a hog's back. Slice the fat in quarter inch slices. Roll in flour. Fry until golden brown.

□ Rev. Wallace Morris

Lard

Drink lard and turpentine for a sore throat.

Pork Sausage

65 pounds of meat, using plenty of fat
 1 pound fine salt
 2 heaping tablespoons of ground sage
 2 heaping tablespoons ground red pepper
 ½ pound black pepper

  Mix well and apply mixture as salt, sprinkling over the meat and mixing well before grinding.

☐ Mary Thomas

Canned Pork Sausage

In days before electric refrigeration, canning was a common preservation method—even for meat.

  Slice sausage into half inch cakes. Fry in black iron skillet. Then cook thoroughly and slowly but leave light brown. Place in hot sterilized half-gallon jars. Have kettle of hot melted lard on back of stove. Ladle melted lard into jar completely covering meat with no air pockets. Partially seal immediately. Place in cold pack (a canning kettle), and cook for 20 minutes. Remove and seal completely. This dish would warm the heart of my family many a cold winter morning.

☐ Susie Burch

Sausage Roast

  The stomach of the hog is cleaned out real good, cut open, and soaked in salt solution; turn inside out. Stuff with some sausage meat. This makes a thing of meat about the size of a big roast. You bake it in an oven. You'd slice that stuff, and it was out of this world.

☐ Marshall Chatelain

Pepper

  Eat a whole peppercorn each day for seven days to prevent chills and fevers.

  Blow red pepper into the nostrils of a woman in labor to hasten childbirth.

Facing page: "Here Mom is putting in a fat piece." Mr. and Mrs. Alford of Roundhill, Edmonson County, grind pork trimings to make sausage, 1972.

Storing Sausage

Salted and spiced sausage would keep for later use if it could be kept cool and protected from insects.

When they made sausage, they would put it in cornshucks. Just shuck the corn and put it in there, and it'd keep for ages.

☐ Mrs. Beckham Hoskins

Sausage in Corn Husks

I hung my sausage in the corn husks on the porch down on the creek. And couldn't no flies get to it. And then when I got ready to cook them, I'd just get up there and take a knife and cut a string and cut them all down. Then take a knife and slice it like you would sausage you buy out of the store. Yeah, they was good fixed that way, and Dad could eat them fixed that way. That's the way I fixed them. I had to. I didn't have no other way. I didn't have no current (electricity).

☐ Hettie Groce

Facing page: "Main Street in Bradfordsville during a turkey drive." The turkeys of eastern Marion County had to walk to market for over sixty years, from about 1857 to 1920.

Bacon Cures

Put a mixture of bacon fat, honey, and flour on boils.

Slices of bacon bound tightly to the back and chest will ease pneumonia.

Singing before Breakfast

If you sing before breakfast, you'll cry before supper.

Cabbage Patch

As independent as a pig in a cabbage patch.

Hopping John

One tradition holds that this dish first appeared being sold by a one-legged street vender named John.

2 cups dried red cow peas
¼ pound salt pork
2 cups cooked rice
Salt and pepper
2 tablespoons butter

Soak peas overnight in open bowl. Cook with salt pork until peas are tender, being careful to keep them whole. Add cooked rice; season with salt and pepper and butter. Cover and simmer about 15 minutes.
Serves 8 to 10.

☐ William H. Dean

Hog Jowl and Black-Eyed Peas

1 pound black-eyed peas
3 pounds hog jowl
3 cups boiling water
1 teaspoon salt

Cover peas with cold water and soak overnight. Cook hog jowl in boiling water for 1 hour. Add drained peas and salt and simmer for 2 hours longer.

☐ William H. Dean

New Year's Luck

To have good luck through the year, make a pair of pillowcases, cook hog jaw, and eat black-eyed peas on New Year's Day.

Snakebite

Place fat pork on snakebite.

Facing page: Restaurant employees pose to have their picture taken.

Country Fried Chicken and Milk Gravy

Also found in the traditional "Biscuits and Gravy," this thick white gravy is a Kentucky staple.

Clean and prepare chicken. Cut into pieces. Let soak in milk or buttermilk 3 minutes. Season with flour, salt, pepper in a paper bag. Prepare deep lard in black iron skillet. Get hot. Dredge chicken in bag of flour. Place in hot fat; brown quickly. Place heavy lid on skillet. Simmer chicken for about an hour, depending on sizes of pieces. Lift lid. Allow chicken to crisp. Remove from fat. Drain on brown paper. Pour off excess fat leaving about 3 tablespoons fat. Blend 3 tablespoons flour into fat. Brown. Add salt, pepper. Pour in the milk you soaked the chicken in. Add more if necessary. About a quart of milk is used in all. Let simmer until thickened. Serve with chicken, hot biscuits, and hot coffee and homemade butter.

☐ Betty Chatelain

Facing page: Fried chicken is prepared for a benefit picnic supper on the grounds of St. Thomas' church near Bardstown, Nelson County. August 1940.

New Year's Dishes

Eat pork on New Year's Day and not chicken, because hogs root forward with their noses and chickens scratch backwards with their feet.

Chicken Remedies

Chicken gizzard tea is good for dyspepsia.

Cut open a chicken and put it on aching feet.

Chicken Protection

Put strychnine, lard, and coal oil on the heads of small chickens to kill lice and hawks.

Water Gravy

As plain as water gravy.

Jay Anderson samples competition class burgoo at the annual international barbeque and burgoo championships in Owensboro, Daviess County, 1982.

Music, Dance, and Burgoo

They used to have square dances here, at each other's houses. In the summer they'd put these platforms on the ground, with plank floors. They'd come from miles off to dance, and lots of times burgoo is what they'd serve because it's quick and easy. Now, my husband was a fiddle player. He loved to have music around him. Lots of times one person would play the guitar, he would play the fiddle, Charlene would play guitar, and somebody else would play a French harp. We'd have a regular hoedown at the burgoo, square dancing and everything.

* * *

They'd have homemade ice cream, cake, and burgoo at these suppers. You could get all you could eat for about twenty-five cents. They'd put them old black kettles out behind the school, sometimes eight or ten of them, and families would come to that supper from miles away, in wagons and buggies and everything. It was just like going somewhere and having supper, you know, they'd socialize a lot.

☐ Helen Francis Jones

Burgoo

Like Brunswick Stew, Burgoo originated as a wild game dish. Burgoo is a thick soup—or a thin stew—made of a variety of meats and vegetables. Recipes for this dish are often guarded as secrets. Burgoo is still a favorite for large gatherings like church suppers.

10 pounds short rib, boiling beef or chuck
 6 large hens or 12 fryers
20 pounds potatoes
10 pounds onions
 4 bunches of carrots
 4 bunches of celery
 4 pounds of lima beans or green peas
 4 pounds of corn
 8 pounds of tomatoes
Black pepper, red pepper, and salt to taste

Prepare vegetables the day before, then cover with water and refrigerate. Cook meat the day before; keep well covered with water. When done, cool and remove from bone and dice. Fill large kettle about ⅓ full with water, then bring to a boil, add meat, broth, chopped and canned vegetables except corn. Add corn in the last 30 minutes. Stir often. When soup starts to thicken, stir constantly. Cook until all fat on the top of the soup has been absorbed. From start to finish, about 12 hours.

☐ Helen Francis Jones

James B. Chapman poses as a hunter, complete with dog and birds, inside a photographer's studio.

Rabbit Pie

Dress and wash two young rabbits. Cut in little chunks and boil in some water. Add a big cut up onion, some bacon fat, and some salt and pepper. Cover pot and cook until it's all tender. Thicken up juice with flour and pour your rabbit pie in a dish of biscuit dough. Bake the pie until the dough is good and brown.

□ Mrs. Charles Sherrard

Rattlesnake

Skin one snake and wash it good. Simmer in water till it's real tender. Season it up and serve it in cream sauce.

Mrs. Sherrard says this has been in the family recipes for a long time, but she hasn't cooked it herself.

□ Mrs. Charles Sherrard

Barbequed Coon

Skin coon leaving fat on back. Place on barbeque pit with back up and cook until tender or until fat on back has cooked away. Salt and pepper as desired. Baste with barbeque sauce while cooking after it has become two-thirds done.

□ Rev. Wallace Morris

Barbeques are a popular Kentucky event. Debates rage over whether a proper barbeque sauce should contain tomato or not, whether to parboil first to retain moisture, and whether to marinade or baste. Owensboro, in Daviess County, is the self-proclaimed barbeque capital of the world and specializes in mutton.

Raccoon Grease

Rub raccoon grease on rheumatism.

Rabbit Brains

Put rabbit brains on the gums of a teething baby to relieve the pain.

A serious cook bastes mutton and chicken with secret barbeque dip and prepares to defend a title at the annual international barbeque and burgoo championships in Owensboro, Daviess County, 1982.

The Meat You Eat

You can tell the type by the meat they eat.

Baked Possum

Skin and dress possum. Boil in salty water for ten to fifteen minutes and drain. Bake with potatoes, carrots, onions, and butter and salt until brown.

Another way to fix possum is to bake it with sweet potatoes and butter. The meat turns out real tender like a newborn baby's skin. This is the reason why Mr. White could never eat possum.

☐ Carl White

Roasted Possum

Skin possum first. Then put salt and pepper all over it. Place in a roasting pan and place in moderate oven. Let cook about two hours. Then remove from oven and take sweet potatoes and completely surround possum with sweet potatoes. Dab butter on sweet potatoes. Replace in oven for about two hours. Remove and pour sugar glaze on sweet potatoes. Cook another thirty minutes.

☐ Rev. Wallace Morris

Possum Hunting

We used to have a dog that when you got ready to go hunting, you made a board the size you wanted the opossum to stretch the skin on, and the dog always caught one the size of the board. One day Ma took the ironing board outside, and we never seen that dog again.

☐ Tom Philpott

Turnip Casserole

Cook one big turnip till tender in salt water. Drain and mash well. Beat one egg into turnip. Add one cup of milk, one tablespoon butter, and two tablespoons brown sugar.

Bake for fifty minutes at 350 degrees.

☐ Mary King

A fish dinner seems to be in store for this gentleman who displays two large carp.

Fish and Milk

Fish and milk eaten together will kill you.

Baked Fish

Fresh fried fish was good in the evening. We liked corn bread and milk, but couldn't drink the milk with fish because it was poisonous.

To bake bass, you put it in a deep pan with tomatoes and butter. Keep basting fish with the hot butter. You put some powder on it, but I don't know what it was. You have to bake it till it almost falls off the bone. Then talk about something delicious!

☐ Marshall Chatelain

Oysters

Never serve oysters during the months with an "r" in their spelling.

Oysters are not good except in months that have an "r" in them.

Pine Bark Stew

This recipe is often served on large smooth pieces of pine bark.

½ pound sliced bacon
5 pounds potatoes
4 cups cooked tomatoes
2 pounds onion
2 quarts water
3 pounds cleaned catfish
1 cup catsup
Salt and pepper

Fry bacon until crisp in large kettle. Force vegetables through a food chopper and add with water to the bacon. Simmer for 3 hours, stirring frequently. Add catfish and continue simmering 30 minutes. Before serving, stir in catsup and add salt and pepper to taste.

☐ William H. Dean

Grease

Drink goose grease and molasses for croup.

Put goose grease in the ear for earache.

Sheep Manure Tea

Sheep manure boiled in water and then strained will break out the measles.

Lemon

Drink lemonade to break out the measles.

To prevent rheumatism, eat a lemon a day.

Hickory

Hickory bark tea can be fed to a mischievious child, but hickory bark works best when applied to the seat of the pants.

Facing page: Outing members make their hunting and fishing camp in the cool of a Butler County cave.

Whiskey Cures

Drink scorched whiskey with bacon grease for indigestion.

For nervousness take whiskey, ginseng, and water.

Take scorched whiskey and sugar for diarrhea.

Hold an open bottle of whiskey against a snake bite.

Sow's Milk

Drink sow's milk for a sore mouth. Better yet, suck on an old sow.

Mint Tea

Mint tea is good for kidneys, for the measles, or for indigestion.

Bed-Wetting

Eat watermelon seeds to prevent or cure bed-wetting.

Cocklebur

Boil cocklebur leaves in sweet milk and feed them to a snakebitten person or dog.

Honey

Drink honey, alum, and red pepper for a cough.

Honey and apple vinegar will help a sore throat.

Honey Bees

No bees, no honey.

Onions

Eat lots of onions for high blood pressure.

Soak an onion in sugar and water; then drink the syrup for colds.

Leave slices of raw onion in a sick room.

Minnow

To cure slobbering, give a baby a minnow to suck on.

Facing page: Beehives made of hollowed-out logs attract tenants at a farm in Stinking Creek on Pine Mountain, September 1940.

Leather Breeches

"Leather breeches," "leather britches," "shucky beans," and "dried beans" are all interchangeable names for the same food—broken, strung, and dried green beans.

We used cornfield beans (striped bean, half-runner bean) that wound around a cornstalk.

You wash them, then you string them and dry them in the sun. Then you take a needle (darning needle type) and a piece of twine and string them up. Then hang them in the sun or close to heat. We usually fixed a rack right behind the coal stove. We had a Home Comfort stove with the heat coming out the back. We hung the beans from nails on this rack until they were dry. Then we'd get a close-wove flour bag and put them away after they were dried.

I don't dry them anymore, I prefer canned beans.

☐ Rovertie Bolen Wills

Facing page: Three ladies lean against a backyard cold frame, a small "greenhouse" which extended the garden's growing season.

Drying Apples

Drying and sulphur-smoking fruits preserved them for use long after their growing season ended. Dried fruit pies were a popular way to serve the leathery dried fruit.

One summer here I dried a whole lot of apples, and I had a place after we moved here, I put a piece of roofing across that porch there and dried them just through the light—just through the sun, in the sun. But I dried them there, put paper on that roofing to keep it. I thought it might blacken, and so I put newspapers on that roofing and dried them apples in there. And spread something over them of a night. Of course at that time they couldn't get no flies in here, you know. You know, flies'll suck all the cider out of apples when you're drying them. And so they never was a fly on them, and they dried the prettiest and brightest you ever seen. And I don't know how many I dried— eight or nine gallon jugs full, though, and I put them in the stove then when they got nearly dry and finished drying them out in a wood stove and then put them in them jars while they was hot, and they never was nothing in them. I could keep them two years at a time that way, yeah. Yeah, they never was nothing got in them. Course they never to start with, cause I kept them, the porch was screened in, you know, and that sunshine hot there from along about nine o'clock till it got late like it is now, and then I could close a window, and that could keep the dew off of them. These windows scoots, and that one does yonder, too.

☐ Hettie Groce

Storing Potatoes

In this clever arrangement, a rock forms the door into a dirt-covered mound of stored potatoes.

Put down dry crab grass first. Then pile on your potatoes. Place a rock at one side of the pile, and cover it with crab grass. Cover the potatoes with lots of dried grass, then with eight to ten inches of dirt. When you want to get some potatoes, just remove the rock. If there is a bank close by, you can dig a hole out of it instead of piling the potatoes on the ground.

☐ Mrs. Naomi Murphy

Storing Food in Caves

We had tables set up in saltpeter caves in Hart County (about four miles from Uptons) and put sweet potatoes, canned fruit, and kept them there. It was warm in the caves in the winter and cool in the summer.

☐ Mrs. Luther Doren Hardy, Sr.

Facing page: Potatoes are harvested in Jefferson County, September 1940.

Ice House

We cut our ice from the ponds. Then my husband would cut it with an axe and drag it off the pond with ice hooks. He usually would haul it away with a sled, and when we got back would put it in the ice house and cover it with straw. That might keep up to May, depending on the amount we had. They would put watermelon and soft drinks and things like that on the ice.

☐ Mrs. Fenton Jett

Ice was frequently stored in a hole in the ground and covered over with a deep layer of straw or sawdust. An ice house could also be a well insulated rock or dirt structure above the ground.

Dropped Dishrag

When you drop a dishrag, it means someone will go hungry.

Dried Pumpkin

We had a large Comfort Cooking Stove. We would first cut up, cut off the rind of the pumpkin and cut it in small pieces, then string it on a string and put it behind the stove to dry. We would also, well that's something else, though. After it was dried, it was ready to make pumpkin pies, or we sometimes would fry the pumpkin.

☐ Alma Hughes

Pumpkin Drying

Pumpkins were peeled and cut into circles, hung on tobacco sticks, and dried outside or in an empty storehouse.

☐ Herschel Lucas

Stored Pumpkins

The insects didn't bother the pumpkins. A mouse sometimes would gnaw on them a little or try to get into the seed, but they didn't eat stuff like that. See, they had a big thick shell. They had sort of a protection, and since it was real hard, nothing bothered it.

☐ Rovertie Bolen Wills

Preserving Peaches

Cover ripe peaches with paste made of gum arabic and two coats of varnish. Simply peel the coating off as though it were the shell of a hard boiled egg.

☐ Eliza Newton

Storing Cucumbers

Pick your cucumbers when they are ripe. If you then dip them into paraffin wax, they will keep indefinitely. When you want to use them, just crack off the wax.

☐ Frances Murphy

Facing page: Corn, grapes, and bean poles are visible as a man hoes in his large garden.

Pumpkin Bread

Milk
Salt
Pumpkin—1 cup
Molasses—1 tablespoon
Meal
Soda

Make into pones and bake.
My grandmother's grandmother used this recipe for making pumpkin bread.

☐ Mary Puckett

Pumpkin Jam

Wash and clean four big pumpkins. Cut up in little pieces. Pour about two pounds of sugar over the pumpkin and keep it out overnight. In the morning, add some dried apricots and about a pound of raisins. Cook all this till the pumpkin is tender and you can mash it up good.

☐ Mrs. Charles Sherrard

Facing page: German prisoners of war load hay on a wagon at the Ewing Galloway farm near Henderson, Henderson County.

Wart Cure

Place blood from a wart on a pumpkin seed and drop the seed into a well or crawfish hole.

Halloween Jack-O-Lantern

Bee came out the other morning to get his little grandson a pumpkin to make a jack-o-lantern out of. And these people that rents our cabin, Mrs. Egton said she didn't think she wanted to fool with a jack-o-lantern, and I told Irene—that's her daughter-in-law—I said, "Irene, you get you one to set on your porch." "Ah," she said, "I'll just put Millard on the porch that night." That's her husband.

☐ Hettie Groce

Gourd Drinking

Drink water from a gourd to prevent rheumatism.

Gourd Guts

As green as gourd guts.

Taters

It's all vines and no taters.

Sweet Potato Pudding

This is a sweet pudding like the filling of a pie without the pie shell.

2 large sweet potatoes, grated
2 eggs
1½ cups of sugar
1 teaspoon of cinnamon
1 cup melted butter
2 cups sweet milk
½ teaspoon of salt

Mix all ingredients together and bake in moderate oven one hour or until it sets. Stir once while baking.

☐ Mrs. Ralph Wilkinson

Facing page: "Mrs. Armitage's Rose Garden" behind the annex to the Morehead Hotel in Bowling Green, about 1900. The two proprietresses, Mrs. Dewey and Mrs. Armitage, stand on the second story porch.

Sweet Potato Pie

Sweet potato pie often resembles pumpkin pie in look and taste. This recipe, however, is more like an egg custard pie.

2 cups mashed sweet potatoes   ⅓ cup butter
½ teaspoon salt   1 cup sugar
4 egg whites, stiff   2 pastry-lined pans
4 egg yolks, beaten   1 cup milk
1 teaspoon cinnamon   ½ teaspoon nutmeg

Mix all except egg whites, well. Fold beaten egg whites in mixture and pour in unbaked pie crust. Bake at 450 degrees for 15 minutes. Turn temperature back to 350 degrees and cook until firm, about 30 minutes.

☐ Mrs. W. Steven Johnson

Vegetables to Sell

It ain't a bit of trouble for me to sell nothing we grow here. Mary told me, "Hettie, what's people going to do when Cord and Hettie quits growing stuff?" I tell you it won't be long till they have to furnish their own gardens, I guess. We could have sold every sweet potato we raised this year. And Irish potatoes, too. There was the awfulest amount of people would come here and ask if we had any potatoes to sell, and I told them we done sold all we had to sell. Looks like they going to have to go to work theirselves, some people, don't it?

☐ Hettie Groce

Wild Greens

We'd start real early in the morning so it was an all day venture. Mother always got a tubful 'cause we all loved them. We'd go to the apple orchard and look for a narrow dock (if you get wide dock, you're in trouble, 'cause it's poisonous) and wild lettuce. Then we'd look around and look for lamb's quarter. Nearby in the meadow we'd find wild mustard and dandelions, poke, and such. Then we'd drag the tub home and wash them and wash them and wash them. And after that we'd pull the stems out of these, and mother would cook them in either a huge black kettle or a copper boiler, depending on the amount. She would put a huge slab of salt pork in them and cook them half a day. And we'd smell those greens and go ape. Then she'd cook cornbread and serve it with them and cold milk. That made a whole meal. In the fall we'd settle for kale and cultivated mustard greens and turnip tops, but they weren't as good as the wild spring greens.

☐ Betty Chatelain

Facing page: "A picnic party on the banks of Drake's Creek... Alex in the rear eating a banana and dangling the peeling on his Aunt Margaret's neck." Near Bowling Green, Warren County.

Sassafras Tea

This tea is also commonly made from the roots of the sassafras tree.

4 pieces of sassafras bark about 4 inches long
5 cups water

Place sassafras bark in water and boil to the desired strength and color. Serve with sugar and cream if desired. Should drink it in February or March. It is a good tonic.

☐ Emma Cunningham

Blackberry Picking

We used to look forward to and dread the dewberry and blackberry season. We loved the berries and pies, but Mother would tie rags dipped in coal oil around our wrists and ankles to ward off the chiggers. When the sun started beating down on the rags, the coal oil smell would permeate all of us, and the chiggers seemed to jump right over the rags while we were berry picking and bit us anyway. But then when we ate the pies, we'd seem to forget all about the chiggers.

☐ Betty Chatelain

Picking Cucumbers

There are many beliefs concerning tasks a woman should not perform during menstruation—making soap, canning, gardening and so forth.

If a woman picks cucumbers at the time of her monthly period, the cucumber vines will wilt.

APPLES! APPLES!—10 bbls. of very large and fine Apples, some of them are Bellflower, very fine. For sale by   COGLE & GRAY.
January 14, 1845.

RAT TRAPS.—We have in store and for sale a few patent Rat Traps.   COGLE & GRAY.
January 14, 1845.

GROCERIES! GROCERIES!

JUST received a large and fresh supply of Family Groceries, consisting in part of
A fine article N. O. Sugar.
    do.   Java Coffee.
    do.   Havana do.
    do.   Old Rio do.
    do.   Sugar House Molasses.
    do.   Plantation   do.
    do.   Young Hyson Tea.
    do.   Gunpowder   do.
    do.   No. 1, Boston Loaf Sugar.
    do.   No. 4,   do.   do.
1 frail Almonds.
50 boxes Star Candles.
10 do Sperm do.
20 do. Tallow do.
15 do. prime Western Reserve Cheese.
1 do. Pine Apple   do.
2 bbls. of Pickled Herring.
15 boxes of prime M. R. Bunch Raisins.
8 hf. do. do. do.   do.
20 drums Smyrna Figs, a prime article.
1 box Chocolate, fresh and fine.
500 lbs. sugar cured Dried Beef.
75 lbs. Venison Hams.
15 bbls. prime Apples.

BALLS, PARTIES AND WEDDINGS.

LEWIS & TODD would inform their friends and the public, that they are prepared to furnish Balls, Parties and Weddings with Cakes, Candies, Ice Creams, Fruits, &c. &c. at short notice, on reasonable terms.
January 1, 1845.

HOT BREAD.

WE will have HOT BREAD every morning, except Sunday, during the winter.
                         LEWIS & TODD.
January 1, 1845.

PIERSON'S HOARHOUND CANDY, for sale by
  Jan. 1, 1845.   LEWIS & TODD.

ROSE ALMONDS, for sale by
  Jan. 1, 1845.   LEWIS & TODD.

CRACKING KISSES for sale by
  Jan. 1, 1845.   LEWIS & TODD.

TOYS in great variety, for sale by
  Jan. 1, 1845.   LEWIS & TODD.

BON BONS for sale by
  Jan. 1, 1845.   LEWIS & TODD.

CANDY of all kinds always on hand and for sale by
  Jan. 1, 1845.   LEWIS & TODD.

CIGARS.—Regalia, Principe, Canones, Panatelas and other kinds of very superior Spanish Cigars, for sale by (Jan. 1, 1845.)   LEWIS & TODD.

DOXON CIGARS, and very superior Common Cigars,

Ginseng

The root of this plant brings a high price because if its alleged restorative and aphrodisiac properties.

Two or three good-sized roots in a half pint of whiskey and a half pint water makes a good tonic for nervousness.

Drink ginseng tea for sex weakness.

Wild Plum Tea

Drink wild plum bark tea for wheezing.

Poke

Although the young shoots of this plant are sometimes eaten as greens, the roots and the uncooked shoots are poisonous to man.

Take poke berries like pills to cure chills.

For indigestion, drink pokeberry wine.

Drink poke root or berries and whiskey two or three times a day for swellings.

Facing page: Advertisements in the Daily Commonwealth, Frankfort, Franklin County, January 22, 1845.

Sassafras Remedies

Chew sassafras leaves for gumboils.

Drink sassafras tea to thin the blood.

Oak Bark

Give white-oak bark tea for children's diseases.

Drink red-oak bark tea for diphtheria.

The inner bark of an oak tree is a laxative.

Mistletoe

Make a tea of mistletoe leaves and drink it for dizziness.

Sweeping before Breakfast

It just isn't to be done, sweeping the floor before you'd eaten your breakfast.

☐ Bessie Ramsey

Hominy

This prepared corn may be eaten with butter and salt as a vegetable dish or may be used in other recipes like Hominy Corn Bread. Hominy is thought to have been originated by Algonquian Indians.

Corn   Lye
Water   Large vat or tub

Put corn in a large vat or tub. Fill with water. Put in a can of lye. Boil until the skin of the corn is loosened and the corn is done. Then rinse over and over again until all of the skin is off and the lye is rinsed off good. Heat the corn and put in cans. Seal.

□ Mary King

Green Corn Pudding

Grate corn until you have three pints. Add to this a cup of fresh milk, two spoons of fresh butter, one spoon of white sugar, three well-beaten eggs, and as much salt as you like. Mix well and pour into a well-buttered dish. Bake for an hour. If it browns too fast, cover pan.

□ Mrs. Aubrey Brookshire

Facing page: Many young hands help with this threshing operation. The crop may be oats to be fed to horses.

Popcorn

We used to fix popcorn cooked in lard, and after eating this, our mouths would be parched. But Mother wouldn't let us drink water after it 'cause we would blow up and pop.

□ Betty Chatelain

Calling Twenty Years Back

Well I can break the corn and throw it in the wagon bed, and he can—and all I can do, it takes some of this work off his hands. And I think when I go and help him I feel better, and if I could go like I once went, I'd go every time he went on the wagon, backwards and forwards. Yeah, that's what I used to do.

And then he said a lot of times here lately he'd just love to call back twenty years of his life. And I said, "Well, Dad, that's just something we can't call back." I said, "It's gone." And it is. But he said, "If I could, I'd just love to call back twenty year of our life." But I told him we just had to take it easy and do the best we could, that's all I know. But he does love to farm. It's a sight how good he loves to work, I don't know.

□ Hettie Groce

Corn Cures

Take corn silk tea for bed-wetting.

Drink cornshuck tea for fever or to break out measles.

Corn Meal Mush

Like Cream of Wheat or oatmeal, corn meal mush is eaten as a hot grain porridge. Cooled, sliced, and fried, it is eaten as a breakfast side dish to bacon or ham and eggs.

½ cup corn meal
2¾ cups boiling water
¾ teaspoon salt

Sprinkle corn meal, stirring constantly, into rapidly-boiling water. Add salt. Cook 30 minutes over direct heat.

For fried mush, pour while hot into a baking powder can or mold which has been rinsed in cold water. Cool until firm. Remove from mold. Slice ¼ to ½ inch thick. Brown in hot fat.

☐ Elizabeth Dunning

Cushie

Crumble cold leftover corn bread into hot grease in black iron skillet. Add enough water to steam crumbs. Brown lightly. Serve with milk gravy on top. Delicious!

☐ Betty Chatelain

Facing page: Children carry a sack of meal home on mule back. Knox County, September 1940.

Grist Mills

We'd take our corn to the grist mills. Some of them had big wheels that was run by water. There'd be a big creek, and they'd dig out a section of it and put boards across it to run it down where they wanted it. And they'd put this big old wheel, similar to a windmill, there, and it would grind the meal. They finally got gasoline engines.

☐ Rovertie Bolen Wills

Hoecake

This pancake-like cornbread is served in place of rolls or biscuits. It is commonly buttered, then eaten with the fingers.

1 cup corn meal   Salt to taste
Milk   Dash of sugar
1 egg

Mix meal and milk in mixing bowl. Mix the milk until it becomes sloppy. Put enough grease in iron skillet to cover the bottom. Add salt and sugar to milk and meal. Place 3 dobs of batter into the skillet and let brown. Turn and let other side brown.

☐ Christine Mallory

Plowing

I love to plow. I always did love to plow, but it's awful hot work, yeah. It is for a woman, now. A man can still stand it better than a woman, I guess. But I love to plow.

☐ Hettie Groce

An eastern Kentucky man grinds corn by hand using grindstones set into a hollow-log base.

The Last Biscuit

A girl who takes the last biscuit from the plate will be an old maid.

Cooking Biscuits

We had no rolling pins, so we'd take and pat the dough in our hands, and we'd cook the stuff in a skillet covered with hot ashes. Food really had seasoning in it when I was young.

☐ Mattie Scott

Hominy Corn Bread

I make this recipe like my corn bread, but hominy is used for flavor. Use a little shortening, two eggs beat up good, and about a cup of milk. Add the hominy and a half cup of corn meal and some salt. Bake the bread in the oven till it's a golden color.

☐ Margaret Altman

Gritted Bread

This is also known as "grated" bread.

Use corn which is too hard for "roasting ears," but not hard enough to parch. Grate the corn on a gritter and use in place of corn meal for corn bread. A gritter is made by making nail holes in a piece of tin, then fastening the tin to a board.

☐ Nora H. Cornett

Hearth Cooking

My stepmother-in-law used to cook on a hearth, and she'd put her a big—big, round sticks, you know, on the hearth. And it's hot there, and she'd bake her bread on that hearth, and that was the best bread you ever eaten. And then she'd get her a kettle and put it right in the middle and cook in that right on that grate and on that hearth.

☐ Mrs. Roxie Gibson Barnett

Moldy Biscuit

Place a molded biscuit, soaked in buttermilk, on a boil.

Rising Bread

If your bread won't rise in the morning, you'll have rain or snow by night.

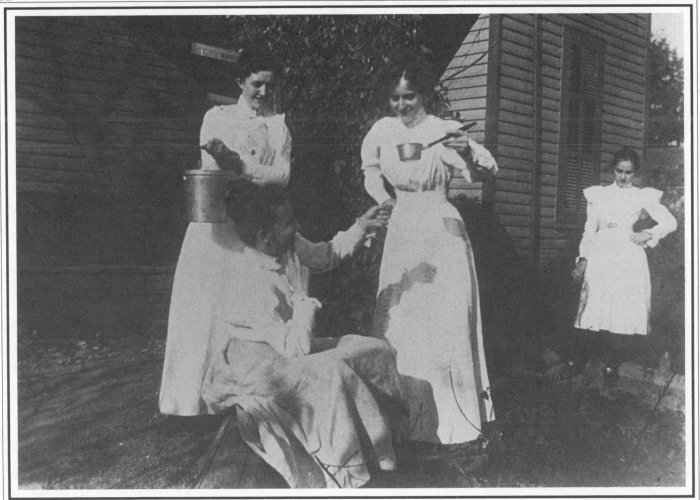

Country Cottage Cheese

You heat the milk very slowly on back of wood-burning stove. If you get it too hot, it will ruin. When milk clabbers all the way through so a knife will cut it, you remove from stove and pour into thin cotton bag. Hang bag, whey dripping out through cloth. When curd is dry, season with cream and salt. Serve. It's delicious. We were raised on it.

☐ Betty Chatelain

Baked Milk

Put the milk in a jar, covering the opening with white paper. Bake in a moderate oven until thick as cream. It may be taken by the most delicate stomach.

☐ Mrs. Joe Veech

Cream

To have a pretty beard, put cream on your face and have a cat lick it off.

Facing page: A cool drink is shared in a summer yard.

Spring-Cooling Milk

To keep our milk from souring, Ma would put it in 2 or 3 gallon buckets and take it and set it under the head of a spring on a big rock. Us kids would take us a pone of corn bread, sneak down to the spring, and eat bread and milk.

☐ Mrs. Ora Davidson

Cellar-Cooled Milk

We kept our milk in the cellar. Our cellar had concrete and limestone. We poured water on the floor of the cellar every morning to keep it cool. Some people had spring houses, but we had an awfully good cellar.

☐ Mrs. Alvin Brooks

Store Bought Milk

But ever since we have been married I've kept milk and butter, and I never did buy bought milk from these here milk companies, nothing like that. I'd buy milk when our cows went dry off of a neighbor that lived down on the Watson Place, Aunt Thursday Watts. But I never drunk a bit of store bought milk in my life, it or no butter neither. But they say when you get used to it, you can't hardly drink the country milk.

☐ Hettie Groce

A sign along a western Kentucky
road advertises honey for sale, 1978.

Churning Butter

Well now, you put milk in the churn and let it thicken. And then it's ready to churn. Sometimes, now, you have to warm it up—set a fire or pour warm water on it, one, to get it warm enough to make butter. Then you churn it till that dash'll stand up on top of that butter, and then you just take it and gather it with the dasher, you know. And you're ready to take it out. And then you take it out and wash it through two waters—I always do. And work all that water out of it, then salt it to the taste I want. And then put it in a bowl, put it in the deep freeze or in the Frigidaire, one, and that just all there is to it. It's just easy done.

And I have churned every day. You know, I'd churn to put up—take up a churning, put in another one. And I'd make anywhere from when we's milking three cows, I'd just take the top of the milk off, the cream. Then I would put that cream in a churn and churn it, and I'd make three quarts of butter. And then have to work it out, you know, and put it in a bowl. And I sold butter, it was awful, yeah.

(What did you used to sell it for? Do you remember?)

To people to eat!
(I mean, how much did you usually—)
I'd get thirty-five cents a quart's worth.

☐ Hettie Groce

Butter Churn

I learned to make butter from my mother and my mother-in-law after I got married. I used to try to churn when I was a child. Mom never let us do it too often. She was afraid we'd beat the bottom out of her churn.

☐ Ruby Russell

Riddle I

"Cream that got fright with a stick"
   (Answer: Butter)

☐ Mrs. James Lincoln Blue, Sr.

Riddle II

"Big at the bottom
Little at the top
Little thing in the middle
Goes flippity flop."
   (Answer: Butter churn)

☐ Mrs. Mattie Frazier

Bobby Hayden and Fred Johnson show off the height of their McLean County sorghum crop in 1976.

Molasses Making

Sorghum is still grown in Kentucky and continues to be used to produce molasses. In earlier times, sorghum molasses provided a cooking and eating substitute for commercially available sugars.

One time Mr. Young and his son went to Indiana to buy some molasses. He said, "This old feller with a long beard came out, and I said, 'Oh Lord, we're at the wrong place.'" They were, however, at the right place. The "old feller" was "makin lasses" using a gas motor despite the fact that he would not allow neither a tractor nor a car on his property. He plowed with a mule and drove a horse and buggy, but for molasses he had nothing but the best.

☐ Harry Young

Immunity

To immunize yourself against poison ivy, drink a mixture of molasses, sulphur, and saltpeter.

Peaches

Give peach leaf tea for worms.

Carry peach leaves in your hat to prevent rheumatism.

Drink peach bark tea sweetened with sorghum for cramps.

Corncob Jelly

12 red corncobs
 2 quarts water
 1 package sure-jell
 3 cups sugar

Boil corncobs in water for 30 minutes. Remove from heat, strain liquid. If not 3 cups, add enough water to make 3 cups. Add sure-jell and bring to a rolling boil and boil 3 minutes. Remove from heat and pour into small jars. Seal.

☐ Mrs. M. Story

Mincemeat

4 pounds pork (cooked, then ground or
   chopped)
9 pounds apples, chopped fine
9 pounds of raisins   5 quarts sugar
1 quart vinegar   1 quart molasses
5 teaspoons ground cloves
5 teaspoons ground mace or nutmeg
10 teaspoons ground cinnamon
5 teaspoons salt
1 teaspoon black pepper
2 lemons, both juice and grated rind

Mix all together, heat until the boiling
point is reached, then seal jars.

□ Mary Thomas

Pretty Canning

I've canned them so that you'd be looking at half-peaches—the prettiest things
you ever saw. Back then, I was particular
about the way they looked.

□ Rovertie Bolen Wills

*Facing page: Josh Calahan's wife displays some of
her canned goods in the cellar of their new home
in the Southern Appalachian Project near Barbourville, Knox County, November 1940.*

Canning Conversation

What you put up used to be a topic of
conversation. I used to take the children's
teachers down to show them the food.
That was just the way of people then.

□ Rovertie Bolen Wills

Food Poisoning

We always heated up everything that
didn't have enough acid in it to take care
of it. Now tomatoes, you can just open up
a can of them and eat them right out of
the can. But all our corn, all our beans we
cooked so you didn't get food poisoning.

They had cans in all the country stores.
They had pints and quarts and half-
gallons. We always washed them good,
and we put them in a scalding solution to
kill all the germs. All of them had to be
done like that.

□ Rovertie Bolen Wills

Storing Apples

We would go out before it got real cold into the orchard. If we were in a hurry, we'd gather up the apples to keep them from freezing, and we put them into burlap bags, and we would put leaves over them. There was just so many leaves, nice, clean and dry. Then, you would put these leaves over the apples on the ground until you had time to put them in the root cellar. It was getting cold enough then so that there weren't no insects to bother them. And the mice usually went to buildings. The fall of the year and early winter was the busiest season, getting all of this stuff put away.

We usually did this with the smaller apples. Later on, we would end up feeding some of these to the pigs. The pigs had to eat, too.

☐ Rovertie Bolen Wills

Cider and Honey

Drink apple cider and honey for colds.

Facing page: Mr. "Patsy" Fitzpatrick, owner of a Bowling Green bar, and two friends give barrel-hauling oxen an extra load.

Sulphured Apples

Drying and sulphur-smoking are two methods of preserving apples for later use. Sulphuring apples is also known as "whitening" them.

I'd go to the tree and pick them up and wash them good and clean and lay them out in the dishpan and then let that water drain off them. And then I'd peel them and put them in a basket, spread me a cloth in the bottom of the basket. And that cloth—when I get that basket full of apples, I turn that cloth right back over the top of it. And then when I get them ready to smoke, I put them in a barrel and put me some fire coals in that barrel and put the sulphur right on top of them fire coals. And that basket is ready to hang over, down in that barrel. Then when I get my basket hung up in there, I spread a sheet over the barrel to keep the odor in there. Then I let them set over night. Next morning I go out and get them and put them in gallon jugs— half gallon jugs or just anything like that. And seal them hard and tight. And then when I get ready to fry them, I wash them, I wash them in warm water twice. Then I let that water drain out and put some grease in the skillet to keep them from sticking. And then I put some sugar on them, fry them down low, and they're delicious! Yeah, they're healthy, too.

☐ Hettie Groce

Switchel

Switchel was traditionally a drink for the hottest summer days and for harvest workers who needed a thirst-quenching liquid.

1 quart cold spring water	½ cup molasses
1 cup cider vinegar	1 tablespoon ground ginger

Stir well. Serves 4.   ☐ Mrs. Bill Jordon

Sugar Whiskey

This is one version of the famous Kentucky moonshine.

 1 bushel corn
50 pounds sugar
 2 gallons of sprouted corn which has
     been dried and cut

Place all ingredients in a 50 gallon barrel. Fill with water leaving 3 inches at the top. Let this mixture ferment for 3 days at 75 degrees room temperature. This mixture is what you call mash.

Place the mash in a large cooking pot. Cover with lid. The lid should have a copper, coiled tube on it called a worm. The worm leads from the inside of the pot to the outside and enters a large container.

Heat the mash until it starts to boil. This will cause the whiskey to come out of the worm. Hold heat at this temperature. The steam coming out of the worm is what changes the mash to whiskey. When steam quits coming out, the whiskey is made.

☐ Anonymous

Facing page: A moonshine still discovered near Glasgow, in Barren County.

So Drunk

He's so drunk he can't lie on the ground without holding on.

Corn Whiskey

Called a whiskey, this recipe really produces a type of beer or home brew.

10 pounds of sugar
 2 boxes of raisins
 1 box of dried peaches
1½ pounds of cut potatoes

1 pound of corn meal
1 can malt
2 cakes of yeast

Place all ingredients in an 8-gallon stone crock. Let ferment for 5 days in a room of 80 degrees. When bubbles begin to rise to the top the mixture is ready to be strained. Strain the mixture through cheese cloth. After the mixture has been strained, it is ready to be bottled. Be sure not to bottle it too soon because it can blow up.

☐ Anonymous

Corncob Wine

Corncobs and sugar are put together in water until fermented. It takes 9 days to ferment it. Strain it, and let it age a very short time. This was very popular with the colored people.

☐ Robert Carroll

Hiccough Cure

Drink ragweed, whiskey, and tansy for hiccoughs.

Always Stir Clockwise

Always stir your batter clockwise. If you reverse the direction, your batter will spoil.

Bourbon Cake

A Kentucky specialty, bourbon is a whiskey distilled from mash containing not less than fifty-one percent corn. Naturally Kentucky cooks developed a cake to show off the state's fine whiskey.

2 cups red candied cherries
1½ cups light seedless raisins
2½ cups firmly packed brown sugar
5 cups sifted cake flour
4 cups pecans
1 teaspoon baking powder
2 cups Kentucky bourbon
2⅓ cups sugar
1½ cups butter
6 eggs, separated
2 teaspoons nutmeg

Combine cherries, raisins, and bourbon. Cover and let stand overnight. Drain fruit, reserve bourbon. Cream butter or margarine and sugar together until light. Add egg yolks and beat well. Combine ½ cup flour and pecans. Sift flour, nutmeg, and baking powder together. Add flour mixture and bourbon alternately to butter mixture, beating well. Beat egg whites until stiff, but not dry. Fold egg whites into flour mixture. Fold soaked fruits and pecans-flour mixture into batter.

Turn into greased 10-inch tube pan lined with greased waxed paper. Bake at 275 degrees for 3½ hours. Cool. Remove from pan. Fill center of cake with cheese cloth saturated with bourbon. Wrap in waxed paper. Store in tightly covered container and keep in cool place.

☐ Mrs. Ralph Thomas

Nutmeg

Eat a lot of nutmeg to cure boils.

Borrowed Salt

It is bad luck to repay borrowed salt.

Facing page: The pleasures of steamboat travel included a shipboard dining room

Kentucky Rum Fruitcake

½ cup butter
1¼ cups light brown sugar
1 cup cheddar cheese
3½ cups sifted flour
½ teaspoon baking soda
1 teaspoon salt
½ cup milk
¼ cup rum
2 cups pitted dates
2 cups walnuts

Beat butter and sugar until blended. Add eggs, 1 at a time. Beat in cheese. Sift flour, soda, and salt together. Add alternately with milk to butter-sugar mixture. Add rum. Beat until smooth. Stir in dates and walnuts. Bake at 300 degrees for 2 hours. Cake may be stored for several weeks in covered container to mellow. Decorate cake with candied fruits for added color.

It received its name, "Kentucky Rum," because it was originally made from rum made on a farm near Summersville, Kentucky, in Green County.

☐ Margaret Altman

Facing page: An afternoon tea was not always a serious affair, as these genteel highjinks suggest.

Orange Peels

Peel your oranges and roll the peels in sugar. Then put them in a jar after you've cut them into small pieces. We used them in fruit cakes. Also lemon peels we did the same way.

☐ Frances Murphy

Batter Stirring

For two people to stir the same cake is bad luck.

Raisins

Eat a teaspoon of raisins with each meal for a month to cure boils.

A sideboard in the apartments above "Patsy" Fitzpatrick's bar on Main Street, Bowling Green, 1900.

The Traditional Wedding Cake of 1855

This is a large version of pound cake, quantities being given in relation to the number of pounds of flour and butter in the recipe.

20 pounds butter
20 pounds sugar
20 pounds flour
20 pounds raisins
40 pounds currants
12 pounds citron
20 nutmegs
 1 ounce mace
 4 ounces cinnamon
20 glasses wine
20 glasses brandy
10 eggs to the pound (about 200 eggs)

Add cloves to your taste. If you wish it richer, add 2 pounds of currants and 1 pound of raisins to each pound of flour.

Fruit cake was the traditional wedding cake in those days.

☐ Mrs. Bill Jordon

Hettie's Wedding

And the day me and Cord's married, his daddy told—there was the awfullest crowd at our wedding you ever saw. Everything on Sulphur Creek was there! And they had an awful dinner fixed. His daddy told some of them that was out in the yard, said, "I ain't got nothing against his wife, but I hate to give him up." Said, "He's the best work hand I've got!" Cord has worked all his life, but he got awful goodly out of it, seem like.

☐ Hettie Groce

Wedding Cake

One pound each of loaf sugar, pounded and sifted; of butter, washed three times and dried in a towel; and dried and sifted flour; twelve eggs, the whites and yolks beaten separately; one pound each of currants, washed in three waters, then dried in a sieve; of best layer raisins, seeded and chopped, and of citron, cut into slips with a pair of sharp scissors; two teaspoonsful of nutmeg and one of pounded cloves; one tablespoonful of cinnamon and a glass of best French brandy. Stir butter and sugar to a cream, beat in the yolks, whipped smooth and strained, and beat steadily ten minutes. Then add, a handful at a time, half of the flour; next the spices, by turns with the other half of flour. Mix with a few quick strokes, always beating upward and in the same direction. Finally stir in the brandy.

This will make one very large loaf or two of fair size. Line a deep tin mold with white paper well buttered and bake steadily for another hour. Take off the paper quickly and shut the door gently not to jar the cake. To shake it would make it streaky.

☐ Mrs. L.M. Davenport

Egg Shells

It is bad luck to throw away the egg shells until after the cake is baked.

Jam Cake

1 cup butter
2 cups sugar
4 cups flour
1 teaspoon baking powder
2 cups jam
5 eggs, beat separately
1 box raisins
1 cup citron
1 teaspoon cinnamon
½ teaspoon allspice
3 tablespoon cocoa
1 cup nuts

Mix and bake in slow oven until done. Keep away from heat to keep moist.

☐ Mary King

Sausage Cake

Mix you up a pound of brown sugar, a pound of pork sausage, a cup of black coffee, and a little soda. Add about three cups of flour, a little salt, cinnamon, nutmeg, allspice, and cloves. Then mix you in a cup of raisins and a cup of nuts. Bake it till it's brown all over.

☐ Mrs. Charles Sherrard

Walnuts

Eat lots of walnuts for mental troubles.

Busy

Busy as a hen with one chick.

Facing page: A family picnic near Chalybeate Springs in Edmonson County.

No-Nothing Pie

6 leftover biscuits
½ stick of butter
1 cup of milk
1 cup of sugar
Dash of nutmeg

Take the biscuits and cut them into halves. Put them in a large pie pan. Add 1 cup sugar, then 1 cup milk, and cut the butter into small squares and arrange over the top. Dash nutmeg over the top. Bake in moderate oven for 15 minutes.

□ Mary Proffitt

Singing at the Table

Singing at the table will be followed by disappointment.

Facing page: A pie's highest bidder enjoys his spoils at a pie and box supper sponsored by the Quicksand School to raise money for needed repairs and supplies. Breathitt County, September 1940.

Bread Pudding

Combine three slightly beaten eggs, one-fourth cup sugar, and one-fourth teaspoon salt. Slowly add two cups scalded milk and one-half teaspoon vanilla. Then take leftover bread (usually biscuits left from breakfast) and break into one-inch size pieces. Stir bread into mixture. Bake at 325 degrees for about thirty minutes.

Rev. Morris said that people used to bake extra biscuits for breakfast so they could have bread pudding for supper.

□ Rev. Wallace Morris

Cooking Dinner

I'll tell you what I'd do. When I's helping him work on the farm, I'd cook dinner, and I had a wood stove with an oven up in it, you know. Well, I'd put what our supper was in the stove and turn the damper off. And of course it's warm weather. Well, our supper would be warm, and I'd be tired, and I'd just come in, and Dad would feed and tend to the stock. And I'd feed the chickens and tend to them and bring the eggs in. And I was so tired I'd always cook my supper when I cooked dinner. And then go back to the field and work from one o'clock you might say to plumb on to nearly sundown. Yeah, that's the way I worked, and that's the way I raised my kids to work.

□ Hettie Groce

Nigger Ed Dumplings

Make biscuit dough as if you were going to make biscuits. Use any kind of fruit you prefer so long as it's easy to cook. For each dumpling, use a piece of dough about the size of a biscuit. Roll it out thin. Spoon out two or three tablespoons of fruit onto the dough. Gather the edges of the dough around the fruit. Pinch the dough together to hold the fruit. Place the dumplings in a deep baking dish. Put a chunk of butter (about one-half inch thick by one inch square) on each dough ball. Add one heaping tablespoon of sugar to each one. Cover with boiling water and bake until golden brown.

This is a family recipe. A slave from a neighboring farm came to my great-great-grandfather's one Sunday visiting. He rushed all the family off to church. He then proceeded to cook dinner. For dessert, he prepared these dumplings. Since his name was Ed, these dumplings have always been known in our family as Nigger Ed's.

☐ Mrs. A.B. Woosley

Facing page: Cave visitors enjoy a picnic in the dark of Mammoth Cave, Edmonson County.

Half Moon Pies

And when canning time came along, he'd pick the blackberries for me in July. And then I'd make my jellies and jams and preserves and dried apples. I don't know how many years here I dried apples. We used to have an orchard over yonder, but it's dead now. And I'd dry apples and sell them and keep what I wanted to use for ourselves. And them apples when they're dried, they make a fine half moon pie. Did you ever eat one?

☐ Hettie Groce

Fried Pies

Have dried peaches or apples cooked and worked or mashed fine and cold. Then roll out ordinary biscuit dough very thin and cut round, the size of a common plate. Have fruit sweetened and flavored to suit taste. Spread the filler on one-half of the dough and turn the other half over the fruit. Press edges together with a fork. Now pierce each pie through and through with a fork and fry a nice brown on each side in smoking hot grease or butter. They are better if turned only once in browning.

☐ Nevelene Herrin

Sugar and Salt

If you have sugar in anything cooking, you should add some salt, too.

Possum Fruit

There's a persimmon for every possum.

Persimmon Cake

2 cups persimmon pulp
½ teaspoon salt
2 cups sugar
2 eggs
½ cup melted butter
2 cups milk
½ teaspoon baking soda
2 cups flour
1 teaspoon cinnamon

Steam persimmons just enough to loosen the seeds. Don't dissolve skins. Run through a food mill to take out seeds and skins. Measure 2 cups. Put persimmon pulp in large bowl. Mix soda with it. Sift the dry ingredients together, then add everything to the persimmons and beat for 5 minutes. Turn batter into greased and floured 8-inch cake layer pan and bake at 350 degrees for an hour.

Especially good with butter cream frosting. ☐ Mrs. Charles F. Schmeal

Facing page: Ladies cool off with a summer picnic of watermelon, about 1910.

Persimmon Pudding

You take your persimmons when they are ripe and run them through a colander to separate the seed and skin from the pulp. Then add some country molasses, sugar, buttermilk, soda, lard, and a small amount of flour. You really have some fine eating.

☐ Dorothy Givens

Persimmons are edible only when they are fully ripe. To assure ripeness, they are generally not eaten until after the first frost. If eaten before they are ripe, the persimmon's astringency will cause the eater's mouth to pucker up uncontrollably.

Soda User

My mother could never live without soda because she used it for everything, and when she would send my brother Pat to the store, if he forgot what she sent him for, he would get soda because he knew she would always use it.

☐ Betty Chatelain

Paw Paw Pie

Paw paws are most commonly eaten raw and plain rather than cooked.

1 cup sugar
1 cup milk
1 egg
¼ teaspoon salt
1½ cups paw paws (peeled and seeded)

Place all ingredients in a stew pan and stir. Cook over medium heat until thickened. Pour into unbaked pie shell and bake until crust is done. Top with favorite topping.

☐ Letcher County ASCS News

Stack Apple Pie

Cook green apples until they are mushy. Add sugar enough to make them sweet.

Make biscuit dough crust, using extra shortening. Roll dough one-half inch thick and fit into an iron skillet. Put one-fourth pound of butter in bottom of skillet before adding dough. Bake fifteen or twenty minutes in a moderate oven. Pour three-fourths inch layer of apples on top of crust. Add a second crust on top of apples and put back in oven until top crust is well done. Pour another three-fourths inch layer of apples over it, then add the third crust and bake.

To serve, cut pie in wedges and top with cheese.

☐ Mrs. Charles Gentry

Coffee Jelly

½ box gelatin soaked ½ hour in ½ teacup
    cold water
1 quart strong coffee, sweetened to taste

Add the dissolved gelatin to the hot coffee. Stir well, strain into a mold rinsed in cold water just before using. Set on ice or in a very cool place. Serve with whipped cream.

☐ Mrs. W.H. Dougherty

Facing page: A backyard chicken coop and a grape arbor are visible in this photo. The evening's main course, however, is open to speculation.

*"Gerrie and Emma selling mud
pies." Woodbury, Butler County.*

Pie Eating

Never eat the point of a piece of pie first.

Chess Pie

2 eggs
¾ cup sugar
1 tablespoon butter
1 tablespoon flour

Flavor with nutmeg. Add sufficient milk for two pies.

☐ Naomi Marcum

Sorghum Pie

4 eggs
1 cup sugar
6 tablespoons cream
2 cups sorghum
4 tablespoons butter
1 teaspoon vanilla

Beat whole eggs together, add sugar, flour, and cream. Lastly add sorghum, butter, and vanilla. Pour in two pie pans lined with unbaked pastry. Bake in slow oven until well done.
Baking time: 45 minutes.

☐ Ida B. Swihart

Buttermilk Pie

2 cups sugar
4 whole eggs
4 tablespoons butter, melted
6 tablespoons buttermilk
1 teaspoon vanilla

Mix sugar, eggs, butter, buttermilk, and vanilla. Pour into unbaked pie shell. Bake in 325 oven for 1 hour.

☐ Mrs. Roy Newbolt

Old Time Meal Pie

Mix you up about a cup and a half of sugar, a tablespoon of meal, and two tablespoons of flour. Cream it together with a half cup of butter, three big whole eggs, some lemon juice, and vinegar. Add your flavoring, vanilla, and beat it all up. Cook in a pie crust for about a half an hour.

☐ Catherine Cantrell

Chess, sorghum, buttermilk, and meal pies are all sweet pudding-like pies without fruits or nuts. They are similar to pecan pies without the pecans.

Sorghum Candy

Sometimes called "Molasses Taffy," this recipe yields a golden-brown hard candy.

3 cups sorghum molasses

Boil until reaches hard ball stage. Drop in water to test it. Divide into as many portions as there are people to pull. Let cool partially until able to handle it. Butter hands. Scoop remaining molasses off plate. After pulling into sticks, put ends together to make ring. Roll over hands until practically cream color. It is this color because it is full of air. Pull into long sticks. Take knife and cut in size desired.

After people quit making sorghum candy, we made sugar candy.

☐ Eula Taylor

Candied Orange Peel

Peel six large oranges and cover the peel with four cups of water and a little salt.

Facing page: A sorghum-making near Jackson in Breathitt County. In earlier days the "stir-off" of the sorghum was a neighborhood event, eagerly awaited by children and adults alike and often lasting into the night as the syrup cooked down.

Weigh the peeling down with a heavy plate and soak it overnight. Drain the peeling and wash it good. Cover the peels with cold water and boil them. Repeat this three times; every time you do, change the water. Cut the peeling up in little strips. Add about three cups of sugar and four cups of water. Stir it all up till the sugar is all mixed up. Cook it till the peel is clear-colored. Drain the peeling and roll it in sugar. Dry.

Mrs. Sherrard still candies her orange peel each Christmas.

☐ Mrs. Charles Sherrard

Candy Making

If you are beating candy and let another person finish beating it, it will turn to sugar.

Glycerin

Take glycerin and rock candy for a cough.

Clear Stick Candy

1 pound sugar
1 cup water
¼ cup vinegar
1 tablespoon glycerin

Cook in skillet usually 20 to 30 minutes or until it was crisp when dropped into cold water. Add a teaspoon of baking soda. Pour onto plates to cool and add 2 tablespoons of flavoring. We quite often spooned it into shallow soup bowls or plates. Each couple had their own soup bowl. We pulled it out in long sticks to the size you wanted it. It can be cut off with buttered scissors, but we usually put it on an old oak table and covered it with an old cloth. You would go around the table in a circle with the candy taking a knife and hitting it to break it up.

☐ Laura Mullins

Facing page: "Candy pulling given by the ladies of Chameleon Springs to Porter Rifles Camp, Christine Bradley, August 22nd, 1898."

Fancy Wrapping

A box of candy was given to a suitor from the girl. The box was chosen for beauty, and if she couldn't find one pretty enough, she bought a box of stationery that was very fancy to put candy in.

☐ Linda Denton

Candy at Christmas

Well, we had a pine tree sitting in the middle of the floor, and we'd decorate it with egg shells. And Andrew was Santy Claus and Jerry was Mrs. Santy Claus. And we strung popcorn around, you know, on string, and put it on our tree. And we'd hang our stockings up, all of us and the children—hang them up on the mantle right by the fireplace. And we'd pour out a big pan full of candy right in the middle of the floor, and the children would get all they wanted. And then they'd hang their dolls and the things on them big limbs of the Christmas tree. And they really had a good time. And it's a true fact—better time than they do today.

☐ Mrs. Roxie Gibson Barnett

All sources cited are in the Western Kentucky University Folklife Archives. Each entry in the following list is arranged this way: (1) name of the fieldworker who collected the item; (2) location of the item in the archives, either by manuscript title and number or, if not separately identified, by the name of the collection in which it is filed; (3) name of the informant, age at the time of the interview, residence, and date of interview. Where more than one informant is listed for one fieldworker, the interviews are numbered. For example Thomas (1) in the source note means that the item was told to Norman Thomas in an interview with the Reverend Wallace Morris.

For many of the sources cited, only part of the above information is available. Each entry has been made as complete as the records will allow, and each is sufficient to locate the source document in the archives.

Banks — Molly Banks, "Appalachian Region Folklore," ms. 1970-72. *Letcher County ASCS News,* 1969

Barton — Catherine Jean Barton, "It's Nothing But a Big Bowl of Soup," ms.

1979-5. Helen Francis Jones, 63, Henderson, Henderson County, 1978

Basham — Marty Basham, Wilgus. Mrs. Bill Jordon, Daviess County, 1961

Blue — Jewell Kay Blue, "Butter-Making," ms. 1971-49.
(1) Mrs. James Lincoln Blue, Sr., 73, Robards, Henderson County, 1971
(2) Mattie Frazier, 76, Robards, Henderson County, 1971

Calvin — Bob Calvin, "A Collection of Food Beliefs," ms. 1972-382. Mrs. Pat Farra, Bowling Green, Warren County, 1979

Chatelain — Marcia Chatelain, "Folklore in Cookery," ms. 1971-11.
(1) Marshal Chatelain, 53, Anchorage, Jefferson County, 1971
(2) Susie Burch, 76, Louisville, 1971
(3) Betty Chatelain, 49, Anchorage, Jefferson County, 1971

Cheek — Larry Cheek, Wilgus. Mrs. Joe Veech, 51, Taylorsville, Spencer County, 1959

Coakley — Cathy Coakley, "Good Old Time Recipes," ms. 1973-166.
(1) Mrs. Charles Sherrard, 54, Rineyville, Hardin County, 1973
(2) Margaret Altman, 53,

Summersville, Green County, 1973
(3) Catherine Cantrell, 62, Summersville, Green County, 1973

Collins — Ronald Collins, in [Ice Houses and Spring Houses], ms. 1978-100. Mrs. Fenton Jett, 74, Cox's Creek, Nelson, County, 1965

Curnutte — Della Curnutte, "Sorghum Production in Green County," ms. 1972-538. Harry Young, 73, Summersville, Green County, 1972

Dailey — Jan Dailey, "Food Storage for Winter Consumption," ms. 1972-5. (1) Namoi Murphy, 75, Paducah, McCracken County, 1972
(2) Frances Murphy, 46, Paducah, McCracken County, 1971

Davidson — Elizabeth Davidson, in [Ice Houses and Spring Houses], ms. 1978-100. Mrs. Ora Davidson, 47, Brandenburg Community, Meade County, 1965

Dean — Margaret E. Dean, "Traditional and Unusual Recipes of Daviess County," ms. 1973-125.
(1) William H. Dean of Harrisburg, Pennsylvania (who was born and raised in Daviess County, Kentucky), 1973

(2) Eliza Newton, Utica, Daviess County, 1973
(3) Mary King, Daviess County, 1973
(4) Mrs. W. Steven Johnson, Daviess County, 1973
(5) Mrs. M. Story [of Daviess County?], 1973
(6) Mrs. Ralph (Mary) Thomas of Owensboro, Daviess County, 1973
(7) Mrs. Charles F. (Nancy Lee) Schmeal of Daviess County, 1973
(8) Mrs. Roy Newbolt of Daviess County, 1973

Dougherty — James E. Dougherty, Wilgus. Mrs. W.H. Dougherty, Bowling Green, Warren County, 1957

Hardy — Barbara Jeane Hardy, in [Ice Houses and Spring Houses], ms.1978-100. Mrs. Luther Doren Hardy, Sr., Hardin County, 1965

Hooe — Laura Hooe, "Candy-Making and Candy-Pulling," ms. 1971-13. (1) Laura Mullins, 51, Bowling Green, Warren County, 1971
(2) Linda Denton, 29, Bowling Green, Warren County, 1971
(3) Eula Taylor, 76, Bowling Green, Warren County, 1971

Houk — Charlotte Houk, "The Country Store," ms. 1972-90. Tom Philpott, 57, Kessinger, Hart County, 1972

Jackson — Barbara Jackson, Wilgus. Mary Puckett, 83, Bowling Green, Warren County, 1961

Lee — Sharon Lee, "Recipes from Relatives," ms. 1974-57. Christine Mallory, 49, Lexington, Fayette County, 1974

Marcum — Joe Marcum, "Folklore Collection Project," ms. 1972-60. Mrs. Naomi Marcum, Woodburn, Warren County, 1972

Martin — Katherine Rosser Martin, "The Preservation of Foods: The Study of a Folk Tradition," ms. 1973-181. Rovertie Bolen Wills, 56, Warren County, 1973

Montell — Montell Belief Collection

Railey — Edna Railey, Wilgus. Mary Profitt, 63, Mt. Hermon, Barren County, 1956

Richardson — Judy Richardson, "Traditional Methods of Food Preservation," ms. 1972-333.
(1) Alma Hughes, 72, Bowling Green, Warren County, 1972

(2) Mrs. Beckham Hoskins, 68, Miracle, Bell County, 1972

Ricketts — Suzanne Ricketts, "Spirited Recipes," ms. 1973-165. Margaret Altman, 54, Summersville, Green County, 1973

Rogers — Martha Ellen Rogers, "Recipes—Sweets with Nuts," ms. 1980-34. Mrs. L.M. Davenport, Greensburg, Green County, 1974

Russell — Judy E. Russell, "Churning and Molding Butter," ms. 1972-343. Ruby Russell, Whitesville, Ohio County, 1971

Shaw — Dennis Shaw, in [Ice Houses and Spring Houses], ms. 1978-100, Mrs. Alvin Brooks, LaRue County, 1965

Spinks — Martha Spinks, "Food Preservation Methods and Associated Dialect from Warren County, Kentucky," ms. 1973-177. Herschel Lucas, 82, Bowling Green, Warren County, 1973

Sullivan — Erin Sullivan, "Moonshine," ms. 1978-16. Anonymous informant, Barren County, 1977

Tackett — Janet Tackett, "Folklore from the Mountains," ms. 1972-524.

Roxie Gibson Barnett, 70, Prestonsburg, Floyd County, 1972

Thomas — Norman Thomas, "Traditional Recipes," ms. 1972-31.
(1) Rev. Wallace Morris, 44, Bowling Green, Warren County, 1972.
(2) Carl White, 51, Bowling Green, Warren County, 1972
(3) Mary Thomas, 51, Bowling Green, Warren County, 1972

White — Linda C. White, "A Dialect Study of an Appalachian Farm Woman," ms. 1973-196. Mrs. Cord (Hettie) Groce, late seventies, Peytonsburg, Cumberland County, 1973

Wilgus — Wilgus Collection.
(1) Emma Cunningham, Cadiz, Trigg County
(2) Mrs. Aubrey Brookshire, 59, Mt. Washington, Bullitt County, 1959
(3) Elizabeth Dunning, Cadiz, Trigg County
(4) Mattie Scott, 61, Owensboro, Daviess County, 1959
(5) Nora H. Cornett, 56, Hazard, Perry County
(6) Dorothy Givens, Quality, Butler County, 1956
(7) Mrs. Charles Gentry, Bowling Green, Warren County, 1959

Wilkerson — Willie Jean Wilkerson, Wilgus. Robert Carroll, White Mills, Hardin County, 1959

Wilkinson — Danny Wilkinson, Wilgus. Mrs. Ralph Wilkinson, Glasgow, Barren County, 1957

Willett — Deborah J. Willett, "A Sorghum Festival," ms. 1972-336. Ida B. Swihart, 45, Hawesville, Hancock County, 1972

Wilson — Gordon Wilson Collection

Wood, G. — Gordon A. Wood, Wilgus. Nevelene Herrin, Providence, Webster County, 1961

Wood, K. — Kenneth Wood, "Folk Beliefs about Food," ms. 1972-380. Bessie Ramsey, 87, Bowling Green, Warren County, 1972

Woosley — Glenda Woosley, Wilgus. Mrs. A.B. Woosley, 51, Roundhill, Edmonson County, 1961

Recipes and Sayings

Page

33 Leather Breeches, Martin, p. 34; Drying Apples, White, p. A-23

35 Storing Potatoes, Dailey (1); Storing Food in Caves, Hardy; Ice House, Collins; Dropped Dishrag, Montell

37 Dried Pumpkin, Richardson (1), p. 18; Pumpkin Drying, Spinks, p. 7; Stored Pumpkins, Martin, p. 62; Preserving Peaches, Dean (2); Storing Cucumbers, Dailey (2)

39 Pumpkin Bread, Jackson; Pumpkin Jam, Coakley (1), p. 47; Wart Cure, Wilson; Halloween Jack-O-Lantern, White, p. A-47; Gourd Drinking, Gourd Guts, Wilson

41 Taters, Wilson; Sweet Potato Pudding, Wilkinson; Sweet Potato Pie, Dean (4); Vegetables to Sell, White, p. A-21

43 Wild Greens, Chatelain (3), p. 68; Sassafras Tea, Wilgus (1); Blackberry Picking, Chatelain (3), p. 32; Picking Cucumbers, Montell

45 Ginseng, Wild Plum Tea, Poke, Sassafras Remedies, Oak Bark, Mistletoe, Wilson; Sweeping before Breakfast, K. Wood, p. 20

Page

47 Hominy, Dean (3); Green Corn Pudding, Wilgus (2); Popcorn, Chatelain (3), p. 3; Calling Twenty Years Back, White, p. A-48; Corn Cures, Wilson

49 Corn Meal Mush, Wilgus (3); Cushie, Chatelain (3), p. 67; Grist Mills, Martin, p. 32; Hoecake, Lee, p. 23; Plowing, White, p. A-45

51 Last Biscuit, Montell; Cooking Biscuits, Wilgus (4); Hominy Corn Bread, Coakley (2), p. 43; Gritted Bread, Wilgus (5); Hearth Cooking, Tackett, p. 11; Moldy Biscuit, Wilson; Rising Bread, Montell

53 Country Cottage Cheese, Chatelain (3), p. 66; Baked Milk, Cheek; Cream, Wilson; Spring-Cooling Milk, Davidson; Cellar-Cooled Milk, Shaw; Store Bought Milk, White, p. A-49

55 Churning Butter, White, p. A-1; Butter Churn, Russell, pp. 10-11; Riddle I, Blue (1), p. 16; Riddle II, Blue (2), p. 14

57 Molasses Making, Curnutte, p. 17; Immunity, Peaches, Wilson; Corn Cob Jelly, Dean (5)

Page

59 Mincemeat, Thomas (3); Pretty Canning, Martin, p. 23; Canning Conversation, Martin, p. 44; Food Poisoning, Martin, p. 65

61 Storing Apples, Martin, p. 60; Cider and Honey, Wilson; Sulphured Apples, White, p. A-25; Switchel, Basham

63 Sugar Whiskey, Sullivan, p. 2; So Drunk, Wilson; Corn Whiskey, Sullivan, p. 4; Corn Cob Wine, Wilkerson; Hiccough Cure, Wilson

65 Always Stir Clockwise, Montell; Bourbon Cake, Dean (6); Nutmeg, Wilson; Borrowed Salt, Montell

67 Kentucky Rum Fruitcake, Ricketts, p. 16; Orange Peels, Dailey (2); Batter Stirring, Montell; Raisins, Wilson

69 Traditional Wedding Cake, Basham; Hettie's Wedding, White, p. A-50; Wedding Cake, Rogers, p. 4

71 Egg Shells, Montell; Jam Cake, Dean (3); Sausage Cake, Coakley (1), p. 35; Walnuts, Busy, Wilson

Page

73 No-Nothing Pie, Railey; Singing at the Table, Montell; Bread Pudding, Thomas (1); Cooking Dinner, White, p. A-42

75 Nigger Ed Dumplings, Woosley; Half Moon Pies, White, p. A-14; Fried Pies, Wood; Sugar and Salt, Montell

77 Possum Fruit, Wilson; Persimmon Cake, Dean (7); Persimmon Pudding, Wilgus (6); Soda User, Chatelain (3), p. 31

79 Paw Paw Pie, Banks; Stack Apple Pie, Wilgus (7); Coffee Jelly, Dougherty

81 Pie Eating, Montell; Chess Pie, Marcum, p. 16; Sorghum Pie, Willett, p. 16; Buttermilk Pie, Dean (8); Old Time Meal Pie, Coakley (3), p. 32

83 Sorghum Candy, Hooe (3), p. 9; Candied Orange Peel, Coakley (1), p. 49; Candy Making, Montell; Glycerin, Wilson

85 Clear Stick Candy, Hooe, (1), p. 3; Fancy Wrapping, Hooe (2), p. 6; Candy at Christmas, Tackett

Photographs

For lovers of Kentucky cooking (and eating), a number of delectable books are available.

Among modern works that tell about foodways in Kentucky's past are two companion volumes by Harriette Simpson Arnow, *Seedtime on the Cumberland* (New York: MacMillan, 1960; reprint edition Lexington: University Press of Kentucky, 1983) and *Flowering of the Cumberland* (New York: MacMillan, 1963; reprint Lexington: University Press of Kentucky, 1984). These books re-create the everyday lives of the ordinary people who settled the Cumberland River basin of eastern Kentucky and middle Tennessee between 1780 and 1803. No aspect of their lives on the frontier has been overlooked—least of all their food (see especially chapter XIV in *Seedtime*). Raymond Sokolov, *Fading Feast: A Compendium of Disappearing American Regional Foods* (New York: Farrar, Straus, Giroux, 1981) has sections on the Midwest and the South that include Kentucky specialties like persimmon pudding, country ham, and hopping john.

Amy Bess Williams Miller and Persis Wellington Fuller, *The Best of Shaker Cooking* (New York: MacMillan, 1970) contains many recipes, supplemented by notes and background information on the cultural and religious life of the Shakers, who had communal homes in Kentucky at Pleasant Hill, near Harrodsburg, and at South Union in the Green River country, near Bowling Green.

Historical essays and many old recipes, as well as newer ones, appear in Dorothea C. Cooper, editor, *Kentucky Hospitality: A 200-Year Tradition* (Louisville: Kentucky Federation of Women's Clubs, 1976), which was compiled and published as a bicentennial project.

Old cookbooks available in modern reprint editions include Mrs. Lettice Bryan, *The Kentucky Housewife* (Cincinnati: Shepard & Stearns, 1839; reprint Paducah, Kentucky: Collectors Books, 1980). Mrs. Bryan's book was designed to guide "[you] who have taken it upon yourself to be a helpmate for your companion, and a guide and governess to those who may be brought up under your care." The introduction mentions, among the duties of such readers, supervising "domestics and slaves." It contains "nearly thirteen hundred full receipts, and many more comprised in many similar receipts." Later in the century, the ladies of the Presbyterian Church of Paris, Kentucky, undertook to "do something more in the way of *benevolence* than was found practicable in the use of the needle." The result was a collection of recipes and household hints entitled *Housekeeping in the Blue Grass: A New and Practical Cook Book Containing Nearly a Thousand Recipes* . . . , new and enlarged edition (Cincinnati: Robert Clarke & Co., 1881; reprint Berea, Kentucky: Kentucky Imprints, 1975).